One Two Buckle My Shoe

Illustrated by Lynne Willey

One, two, buckle my shoe.

Three, four, knock at the door.

Five, six, pick up sticks.

Seven, eight, lay them straight.

Nine, ten, a big fat hen.

One Two Buckle My Shoe

One, two, buckle my shoe.

Three, four, knock at the door.

Five, six, pick up sticks.

Seven, eight, lay them straight.

Nine, ten, a big fat hen.